Carla Holtermann

TRUSTFUL
LIVING

FLEMING H. REVELL COMPANY
OLD TAPPAN · NEW JERSEY

Copyright © 1969 by Fleming H. Revell Company
All Rights Reserved
Library of Congress Catalog Card Number: 69-20147
Printed in the United States of America

Preface

In this age of confusion and restlessness there is one source from which to draw inner quiet and direction. This source is an intimate acquaintance with Him who is our Helper and Guide. Hand in hand with trusting Him goes trustful living. Somehow, as I observe the crowds on our streets, I seem to hear the cry of Job, "Oh, that I knew where I might find Him." Even many who have been instructed in the faith have very little certainty and therefore very little trust. My fervent desire is to hold up to them the one great certainty of faith, Jesus Christ, who is the same yesterday and today and forever, so that they may walk through life confidently affirming, "I know that my Redeemer lives."

Carla Holtermann

Contents

I
TRUSTFUL LIVING

1—Certainty of Faith

"That thou mightest know the certainty of those things, wherein thou hast been instructed" (Luke 1:4, KJV).

If I were writing this book in the form of poetry, I think I would do as did the Hebrew poets of the Book of Psalms, and use their effective teaching device which experts on literary technique call "parallelism." I would say:

O how happy is the person
      who knows in Whom he believes
      and why he believes,
How unhappy is the person
      who only wishes that he could believe,
      and who seeks the answers to so many questions.

For everywhere we see around us these two parallel, but contrasting, kinds of persons—some with nothing firm to grasp, and others with that inner strength that comes from certainty of faith.

"I know *whom* I have believed. I am His. God can use me!" Can you say this? That is what is meant by certainty of faith.

As I travel from city to city throughout this land, it is a continual sadness to me to find how many people don't

7

have this wonderful certainty within their hearts. Everywhere I find a great hunger, a reaching out for something nobler, something divine, something outlasting life. I find this hunger at every age level, every station in life, everywhere—and hunger hurts!

Many are the experiences of this hunger which have been shared with me in private conversation during my travels, and often I have been taken considerably by surprise. For the strange thing is that so often we cannot tell whether someone is living a life of certainty, or one of doubt or indifference. In our culture, we learn early in life to act as if all were well, and to cover up what is really going on inside. Sometimes we come to church outwardly at peace—but inwardly at war. We manage to put on such a happy front, even when our life is empty and defeated. We can look so respectable on the outside, when all the time we know how much evil there is within. We act—at least in church—as if we were so sure in our faith, even when we do not know how to breathe a prayer. We don't dare go for help, because we're so concerned about what people would think! And so year after year this hurt and emptiness and lack of certainty goes on.

When I think of someone who embodies a certainty of faith, I always recall a gracious gentleman, a Greek doctor who lived many years ago in a faraway land. He was a very kind and concerned person—I am sure of this because I have read a letter he wrote to a good friend. That letter must have moved the friend deeply, for into it the doctor put something that breathes of concern and goodness, something that brings healing to me, whom the good doctor certainly never realized would read those words.

It is strange what letters can do to us! In every letter we write we send forth an influence either for beauty or for hurt. I used to scribble hurried notes and sign them, "In haste," easing my conscience with the thought that at least I was letting the recipients know I was thinking of them, and that my haste excused the fact that I hadn't given enough thought and time to the message. I did this often—until one day a letter came to me, signed "In haste." I was already pressured with duties, and those words added to the weight of my breathless pursuit. I determined that never again would I pass on my own tensions in that way to a reader who didn't deserve such treatment.

The letter written by that Greek doctor is not like that; it speaks of quiet contemplation, of time to think things through. He begins, "It seemed good to me to write." This makes me feel good, too, and eager to read on. Then he indicates that he has given previous thought to the content of his letter. He writes, "I am giving you an orderly account" of something very important; not just a hurried jotting down of some facts, but something which will be helpful. Then he boldly makes the statement of what the letter is to accomplish: "That you may know the certainty of those things wherein you have been instructed." The writer of that letter, of course, was Luke, the beloved physician, and the letter was intended to bring certainty to Luke's friend, Theophilus. It has brought certainty to me, and to millions of others who have read it. Its message lives on.

Paul, another early letter writer, speaks of the same certainty. In a letter to Timothy, a young man whom he had brought to the faith, Paul says, "I am not ashamed [of my suffering for Christ], for I know whom I have believed, and I am sure that he is able to guard until that Day what has been entrusted to me" (II Timothy 1:12). Do you sense the warmth which Paul brings with those words, *"I know"* and *"I am sure"*? Not a breath of uncertainty is there. Paul *knows*.

I am glad he used these words, and I am also glad that he spoke of *whom* and not *what* he believed. His source of certainty was not a creed, not a ritual, but a Person, his Lord Jesus Christ. How eloquent is Paul's letter to

9

the Roman Christians, and how full of assurance: "For I am sure that neither death, nor life, nor angels, nor principalities, nor things present, nor things to come, nor powers, nor height, nor depth, nor anything else in all creation, will be able to separate us from the love of God in Christ Jesus our Lord" (Romans 8:38-39). Here, too, lies the source of my certainty. My faith is not built on good advice about how to improve my life, but on the good news of the One who came to redeem my life and to dignify it with His call to discipleship.

Often in my travels I find myself listening to the conversations of men sitting near me at crowded lunch counters, or standing in line awaiting the departure of some plane. There is a saddening sameness to so many of those conversations: prices and profits, gripes, lost hopes, the monotony of life, a tiring routine. I can't help wondering whether some of those men don't long, perhaps unconsciously, to know whether there isn't more to life than this. I wonder if they ever ask themselves, "Is this all life offers? Isn't there more to life than going to work with tensions, coming home with more tensions, watching the TV news report world tensions, going to bed with a tranquilizer and waking up again the next day with a feeling of numb futility? Isn't there something better planned for us, something more than trying to make a living? What is there for our inner longing? *What is it?* Where is it to be found?"

I want so to hold out the healing words of Christ, " 'I am the bread of life; he who comes to me shall not hunger . . .' " (John 6:35) . . . " 'Blessed are those who hunger and thirst for righteousness, for they shall be satisfied' " (Matthew 5:6). Then I realize how strange this all is! The word "blessed" means happy—am I to tell a man that he should be happy if he is hungry for something which seems to elude him? No, Christ did not imply that! He said that a man will be happy when he is fed with the bread of life. But how am I going to help a hard-headed businessman understand what that phrase means?

We must remember that God works with us as individuals, and that there is no one answer to this question; there is no one way to define and declare. Each of us who has experienced Christ as the bread of life must find his own way of telling what that means.

This is how I tell it: The bread which our families eat is physical food from which our physical bodies gain strength. In like manner, Christ is spiritual food for our spiritual beings; we take Him into our heart and life and from Him gain strength for our inner life. When we want physical strength, we do more than just sample crumbs of food; we eat an adequate amount of it daily. Thus, too, if we want strength from Christ we must do more than sample Him, or admire Him from a distance, or occasionally remember Him—this would be a starvation diet. We need daily, full contact with Him.

But how do I answer the friend who asks me, *"How do I accept Christ as my food?"* Again I must refer him to Christ's own words: ". . . he who comes to me." In other words, as we come to Him, we are fed. He invites us to come, to look up to Him, to talk to Him, to listen to Him, to ask of Him and receive of Him. It means walking with a Friend. It's that simple!

And yet it requires so much of us! It requires that we yield our wills to Him, that we be willing to come. It requires that we be humble. We must be willing to admit that we need Him; we must respond to His love and thank Him; we must receive what He wants to give. This requires a decision: Will we or won't we give Christ the chance to feed our hungry longing? It is so tragic to see men refuse or put off this decision year after year until they no longer hear the whisper, "Why be hungry? Come to Me!"

I know a man who, after years of struggling to climb

11

the ladder of success, arrived at last at the top rung. He was executive director of a large corporation, a man of great importance in his community, known for his generosity to his church and to worthy causes. He liked knowing that the employees of his firm called him "the big boss." What more did he need? He had made it to the top!

But this was only a facade, beneath which was a lonely man. At the same time that he loved the praise of men, he feared to take a stand because he could not take criticism. He had developed no close friends, no nearness to his wife and children. Outwardly he was a huge success, and inwardly, a miserable failure.

Fortunately, a day came when he toppled from his ladder. He had been unusually arrogant at work, and a junior executive had "told him off." This made him furious. The crowning blow to his damaged ego came when someone exposed an error which he had made. He went home tense and disgusted, and estranged his family even further by unkindness. In turmoil, and utterly defeated, he fled to his room. There, in stillness and solitude, he eventually quieted down enough to do some straight thinking. He took an honest look at himself, and did not like what he saw: a selfish, praise-seeking coward.

This was agony. It was a death blow to his self-image, but it was also the beginning of a new life. For the first time he dared admit to himself that he was a fraud. Angrily he said to himself, "What am I, a good guy admired by all? No, I'm a phony, and I hate this make-believe stuff." He looked so small in his own eyes, so ridiculous, even despicable. Oh, why had he not seen this before he had made such a fool of himself! A great sense of guilt overcame him as he thought of the coldness of heart and the unkindness he had shown at home and in the office. Crushed, he finally knelt down and in total honesty laid the whole dirty mess at Christ's feet. All he could say was, "Oh, Christ, forgive me. I hate what I am. Help me!"

At that moment the miracle occurred. He had come to Christ, and Christ came to him. He ate of the Bread of Life, and was satisfied. Now he knew at first hand, and for certain, the blessedness of those who come to Christ. Wonderful peace flooded his soul, a peace which he had never felt before, and which he could not understand, but which assured him that he had had contact with God. Again and again he thanked God. He was actually receiving and accepting what God had been offering him throughout the long years, the forgiveness and certainty for which he had never felt a need before.

This change, so real and wonderful, was not only for the moment. From that hour on, he responded to God's love, and grew more and more willing to have his old self pushed aside. Now his eyes were open to the human need all around him. When he returned to his office, his arrogant swagger was gone. His associates were surprised at his warmth and sincerity. Contact with Christ had put him into contact with his fellow men. From *certainty of faith* had come newness of life, inner strength, and direction for service to God and man.

2—Truly Believing

I believe in God the Father Almighty

As we go in search of trustful living we need to distinguish clearly between a nebulous belief in a "higher power" and a belief in the Father-God who is presented to us in the eternal Word of God.

Some time ago I was asked to speak to a group on the topic, "a sure message for a changing world." This was a real challenge for me—in the space age with its constant expansion and its unbelievable changes even in values.

Here was a group seeking to be reassured of something unshakable, something firm in which to put their trust.

To what could I take them which remains constant? What authority could I consult? Immediately there came to my mind the great declarations of Christ: " 'All authority in heaven and on earth has been given to me . . .' "; " '. . . Heaven and earth will pass away, but my words will not pass away' " (Matthew 28:18, 24:35). How refreshing, how unequivocal!

Now I asked myself how I could define this unchanging word. What is it? Peter gave me the answer: " '. . . the word of the Lord abides for ever.' That word is the good news which was preached to you" (I Peter 1:25). What a wonderful way to define the word—the *good news!* With enthusiasm I went to that group and spoke to them of "An Unchanging Christ and His Unchanging Word in a Changing World."

The Apostle Paul calls this good news the *gospel.* He writes, ". . . I am not ashamed of the gospel of Christ: for it is the power of God unto salvation to every one that believeth . . ." (Romans 1:16, KJV). On this gospel we, too, base our faith. This is the certainty on which we stand. Here we meet Him whom we can trust, now and through all eternity.

Coming down to us from the eighth century is a short, concise statement of what the gospel is. Like a clear stream of refreshing water, it has flowed down through the centuries among God's people. In every decade, in all lands, as Christians have gathered together they have strengthened each other's faith and praised God by saying together, *"I believe in God the Father Almighty."* The statement to which I refer, as you already know, is the Apostles' Creed, not written by the apostles but rooted in apostolic teaching. This statement embodies the sure foundation of our faith from which we gain certainty for trustful living.

Let us now concentrate for a moment on how this statement of faith can help us live trustfully. This will be not a theological discussion, but the effort of one layman speaking to other laymen about what life is like when we live as if we believe that there is a God who is our Father. It is one thing to say on Sunday morning in a church building, "I believe in God the Father Almighty"; it is quite another thing to take what we have said out of the church into our homes and offices and shops, and to act as if we really do have a heavenly Father whom we can trust. This faith must work as well on Monday, Tuesday and every other weekday as on Sunday.

Early in Christ's ministry, crowds began to follow Him because they sensed that He cared, and that He had something good for them. "Seeing the crowds, he went up on the mountain . . . opened his mouth and taught them" (Matthew 5:1-2). In His great Sermon on the Mount Christ used the words, "your Father" or "your heavenly Father" fifteen times. He kept repeating it. Finally, when He taught the people how to pray, He said, " 'Pray then like this: Our Father . . .' " (Matthew 6:9).

He made it abundantly clear that we are the objects of a heavenly Father's love. He created us and loves us more than any earthly father can. We are to be happy members of His family, secure in His protection. He wants us to act as if we knew that we are never alone, never have to worry about daily necessities, because " '. . . your heavenly Father knows that you need them all' " (Matthew 6:32). But He does ask us to trust Him one day at a time: " 'Therefore do not be anxious about tomorrow, for tomorrow will be anxious for itself. Let the day's own trouble be sufficient for the day' " (Matthew 6:34).

Once, after I had spoken to a group about the art of trustful living, a woman said to me, "I wish I could live trustfully one day at a time. With my hectic household, I am glad to live trustfully from one crisis to another, with the hope that I'll see the end of the day still trusting."

Step by Step

He does not lead me year by year,
   Nor even day by day,
But step by step my path unfolds;
   My Lord directs my way.
Tomorrow's plans I do not know,
   I only know this minute;
But He will say, "This is the way,
   By faith now walk on in it."
And I am glad that it is so;
   Today's enough to bear:
And when tomorrow comes, His grace
   Shall far exceed its care.
What need to worry then, or fret?
   The God who gave His Son
Holds all my moments in His hand
   And gives them one by one.
              —Barbara C. Ryberg

Another woman once said, "It must be wonderful to live trustfully, but how do you begin to get such trust?" The way to begin is to learn to know Him. You cannot trust an unknown deity. The Bible is the place where you learn of His love for you. Look for His promises that He will love you always, no matter in what condition you come to Him. Underline these promises in your Bible; copy them on a card to carry with you; memorize them so that you can hold them in your heart throughout the day. Whenever doubts and fears arise, repeat these trust-thoughts to yourself, and with them dissolve fear-thoughts.

Before reading the Bible, always remind yourself that God is trying to say something to you personally. Pray, in your own words, a prayer something like this: "Heavenly Father, You are trying to speak to me through these pages, and often I find it difficult to understand. Help me to get

16

your message." Then read, *expecting* to learn something helpful. God will speak to you through the printed words!

An *upward look* the first thing upon awakening to a new day is most helpful for trustful living. Before you open your eyes or speak to anyone, think of your heavenly Father and breathe a prayer of thanks for a night of sleep, thanks for the new day, thanks that He promises to be with you every moment and to help and strengthen you. Then get up and face the day, fully anticipating that it will be good. This will keep you thanking your heavenly Father all day, and you will have begun *trustful living*.

3—Redeemed Living

I believe in Jesus Christ, His only Son, our Lord

"But is that all there is to being a Christian—to live trustfully?" a friend once asked me. No, there is definitely more to it than that. Another aspect of the Christian life is to *live redeemed*.

As Christians, we believe in a Redeemer who suffered and died, arose and ascended into Heaven, and who will return to judge. This Redeemer is Jesus Christ—God in human form—who walked upon the face of the earth to experience all that we must experience, to know all the troubles which we know, to overcome the kind of things which we must overcome, and finally to accomplish our redemption on the cross.

"But these are only big words to me" my friend continued. "I need more than words!" How very true this is. We need more than words; we need the Person, Jesus Christ Himself. And we need a close relationship to Him, an awareness of His abiding presence.

A number of terms have been used to describe this rela-

17

tionship. You might check this list to see which speak to your heart:

One person speaks of an *encounter* with Christ, of crying out to Him in desperate need, in aloneness, emptiness, helplessness, and of then experiencing a great sense of His help and nearness.

Another person speaks of *commitment,* of yielding himself completely to Christ—body, mind, spirit—and accepting Him as Master and Lord, willing now to do what Christ wills for his life.

The word *surrender* is precious to others. They refer to a giving up of self-will and evil, and of letting Christ take over to make them new creatures.

The word *response* makes clear to others man's relationship to Christ. We respond to love. He first loves us, and then we respond by loving and serving Him.

Our Lord Himself often described the relationship as *abiding in Him.* This means constantly living in the awareness of belonging to Him, instead of merely having an occasional thought of Him or a sudden, quick cry for help.

Walking with a Friend is an expression which reminds us that our relationship with Him is not one of trying to keep rules, but of wanting to do only what would please Him as we walk together through life.

Accepting Him as personal Saviour from sin is perhaps the most frequently used and best loved by those who are conscious of having been set free from sin and guilt; it is the least appreciated by those who feel no need of redemption.

This is something that distresses me deeply—the utter unawareness many people have of sin and of the resulting need of redemption. Even many church-going people have revealed to me every level of insensitivity to sin and guilt, and therefore no sense of the need of a Saviour.

I remember a taxi driver who involved me in conversation. After learning that I was on my way to lead Bible studies at some conventions, he proceeded to give me his own religious orientation: "I'm not a sinner. I don't need a Saviour. I can save myself. I have never cheated anyone nor hurt anyone. I'm jolly, and I like people. Everyone likes me. When I go to bed I say to myself, 'I've been a good Joe today,' and then I go to sleep." With no sense of personal sinfulness, he rejected all thought of needing a Saviour.

Let's go back to the statement, "I'm no sinner . . . I have never cheated anyone nor hurt anyone." These words reveal total ignorance of sin as being separation from God, estrangement from God, indifference to God or total neglect of God. So many individuals are unaware that this is the greatest sin. In dealing with persons who ask about a redeemed life I have learned to point to a sinner's need of a Saviour, and to ask how much attention they pay to Him. They need more than words; they need a daily experience of being reconciled to God through Christ. They need to admit that they are by nature sinful and unclean, and that they have sinned by thought, word and deed; that they have sinned not only by outward wrongdoing, but also by secret thoughts and desires which they cannot fully understand but which are all known to Him. They need to ask forgiveness—and afterwards, they need to be told to act as if God had actually freed them from their guilt, and to thank and praise God for this great mercy, even if they are not aware of any special exalted feeling.

To live redeemed means also liberation from any habit, emotion or situation which holds us captive. We need not be at the mercy of any evil. Our Redeemer is not only *on* our side, but *by* our side. At any time, day or night, we may reach for His help.

Are you at the mercy of a quick temper? Bring this to Him and let Him give you self-control. Is it jealousy? Tell Him all about it, and accept from Him the capacity for pleasure in your neighbor's success. Is it worry? Face it realistically, admit your fear, remind yourself of His promises to help you, and let Him perform the wonder of seeing you through, or of giving you strength to grow spiritually within the situation. Is it lack of courage to do the right thing because it is difficult, perhaps even humiliating? Look up to Him, let Him loose the bonds of failure and pride, and make you victorious.

All these helps He gives one day at a time. Redeemed living is never a goal reached—it is a goal approached. Life is growth. Promises of liberation abound in the Word. Find them, repeat them to yourself, and begin to act as if God were leading you onward and upward, step by step. Thank Him in advance for all that He will do for you, and is even now doing in you, even though you may not be able to distinguish it yet. You will then have taken your confession, "I believe in Jesus Christ His only Son our Lord," with you out of the church building and into your own daily world. You will have entered into *redeemed living*.

4—Empowered Living

I believe in the Holy Spirit

Recently I was in the home of a Christian couple, who were active members of their church. Conversation was animated, much of it centering around the new church edifice, the congregation, and the pastor. I could tell they felt real loyalty and love for pastor and flock. During a lull in the conversation, my host looked at me inquiringly and said, "Carla, I am going to confess something to you, and maybe you can help me. I hate to admit it, but I don't know what to do with the Holy Spirit. I know that I believe in God the Father, and I know that I believe in Jesus Christ as my personal Saviour, but what in the wide world am I supposed to do with the Holy Spirit? Every Sunday I say with the congregation, 'I believe in the Holy Spirit,' but it bothers me because I am only saying words without meaning. Please tell me what this is all about." I agreed with him that many persons are not clear about the function of the Holy Spirit in their lives, and that it is good to admit it and to seek clarification.

Before we can come to certainty of faith regarding the Holy Spirit, we need to know who He is. Notice, I do not say "it," but "He." Let us go back to the concept of God the Father. The Apostle John wrote, "No man has ever seen God" (John 1:18, I John 4:12), and "God is spirit" (John 4:24). Because these are words which I cannot grasp, I might fear such an incomprehensible, almighty, unseen God were it not that He kept sending messages of love to His people through the prophets and psalmists. How wonderful are such pronouncements of love: "I have loved you with an everlasting love; therefore I have continued my faithfulness to you" (Jeremiah 31:3); "For the mountains may depart and the hills be removed, but my steadfast love shall not depart from you, and my covenant of peace shall not be removed, says the Lord who has compassion on you" (Isaiah 54:10).

When the time came for God to prove His love for His sin-enslaved children in a visible way, and to rescue them, He took on another form in which He could identify Himself with mankind, so that men could look into His face and see divine love. ". . . though he was in the form of God . . . [he] emptied himself, taking the form of a servant, being born in the likeness of men. And being found in human form he humbled himself and became obedient unto death, even death on a cross" (Philippians 2:6-8). As God-in-human-form He lived among men, teaching and demonstrating God's concern for His children. Finally, on the cross, He took care of our sin-problem. In the crucifixion men saw how much God loved the world (John 3:16). Then men witnessed His resurrection and ascension. His assignment completed, He left this earth. After His ascension, His disciples everywhere kept right on talking to Him, although He was now invisible and they no longer could hear His voice with their ears.

Now a new phenomenon occurred. Before His ascension this Christ, knowing our human loneliness without God's presence, promised to return, not in human form but in a form in which He could invade and indwell each of us at all times—in other words, as the Holy Spirit. Thus the Holy Spirit is Christ come back among His people, in a union with each one of them, His Spirit united with their spirit. We cannot see the Holy Spirit as men could see Christ, but we can know with all certainty when He is at work in our hearts. The Apostle Paul marveled at the thought of our "housing" God, the Spirit. Twice he wrote of it in his letters: "Do you not know that you are God's temple and that God's Spirit dwells in you?" (I Corinthians 3:16); "For we are the temple of the living God" (II Corinthians 6:16).

How could the Holy Spirit begin working in us when we didn't even know who He was? Perhaps we didn't know Him, but He knew us, and He knew the longing of our hearts. He made His presence known to us to bring us comfort. As long as we do not deliberately reject Him, we have His presence within. He abides within us as we willingly submit to His work within us. He builds into us what Paul calls ". . . the fruit of the Spirit . . . love, joy, peace, patience, kindness, goodness, faithfulness, gentleness, self-control" (Galatians 5:22). In other words, this is God in a life-changing activity. He can change us when we give Him the right-of-way.

We are not only to say the words, "I believe in the Holy Spirit"; we are to expect Him to help us in our daily living. We are to live as though there is *One* indwelling us who will help us in every decision. Even though we might not always understand His urgings, He will check us and stop us short before we go too far afield. With gentle persuasion, or with the mighty thunderings of a guilty conscience, with good desires placed in our hearts—in a multitude of ways, He is constantly at work to protect, to guide, to comfort, to bless. Thus, God's power released in us enables God to use us for good in this evil world. Here, then, is the secret of *empowered living.*

5—*Loving Living*

I believe in the Holy Christian Church, the Communion of Saints

One day in the year which always stirs my soul is the World Day of Prayer. Coming as it does on the first Friday after Ash Wednesday, this observance fits so well into the mood of Christ's words, ". . . it is written, 'I will strike the shepherd, and the sheep of the flock will be scattered'" (Matthew 26:31).

On this Day of Prayer I can visualize, more clearly than at any other time, the picture of one Shepherd and one flock. In my mind's eye I see the church on its knees. Beginning at the first flash of dawn in the area of New Zealand, Australia, Japan, women arise to meet for prayer. As the light comes farther and farther across continents, the women of Asia and Europe in turn wend their ways to places of prayer. Finally, when it is already night in the Far East, the Christian women of Alaska and the Aleutian Islands meet to pray. Like telephone lines, reaching from each remote hamlet and island and from the vast metropolitan areas, the prayers of all the faithful rise to the Almighty.

On this day the differences which we Christians have in regard to forms of worship, church government, and individual understanding of some of Christ's teachings—differences which have kept us apart and divided for so long —are minimized. On this day the fact of our oneness in Christ, Our Saviour and Lord, is affirmed. Our awareness of the towering unity in our mutual possession, the living Lord, is enlarged. We are reminded that we all have one book, the Bible. We use the common symbol of redemption, the cross. We observe the same sacraments, baptism and communion. We have the same hope of eternal life. We carry the same family name, Christian. On this day I understand a little bit better that the church is God's human family. He is the family Head. We belong to Him, and therefore we belong to each other.

Why should I say at Sunday morning services that I believe in the church, and in the communion of saints, which is God's family, and then turn around and forget that the believer of another race is just as much a child of God as I am? The word "communion" helps us. The church includes all who share a common possession, a common love of the Lord Jesus Christ. Thus we sing: "In Christ there is no East or West, In Him no South or North; But one great fellowship of love throughout the whole wide earth. Join hands, then, brothers of the faith, What-e'er your race may be. Who serves my Father as a son is surely kin to me."

The word "saints" does not here mean perfect persons. It means believers who, with God's help, want to walk worthy of Him. None of us is worthy of being part of the family. He adopts us just as we are, and changes us more and more into His likeness. What we have in a local congregation is a cross-section of the whole church upon earth, with all levels of need, defeats, failures and victories.

24

Here we have fellowship imperfect and temporary, the church militant. One day we shall enjoy the fellowship with the church triumphant.

We speak in the creed of the holy church. The word "holy" does not mean perfect or sinless. It means set aside for God and His service. It means a gathering of all who are willing to do the work assigned by their Lord; namely, to scatter love and goodwill, to intercede for each other and the world, to share Christ with those who do not yet know Him.

On the World Day of Prayer I realize again that the forces of the world are too strong for a divided church. We dare not quarrel and hinder each other in leading men to the Saviour just because we have some differences in understanding. Christ's act of redemption is, after all, the divine fact to which we all can hold. As defenders of the faith we need to resist, in unity, the cunning and deceit of the principalities and powers of evil.

We have a task to do! We are to be ambassadors for Christ, workers together with Him. I find frightening the fact that every day, even every hour, we Christians are losing ground in the evangelization of the world. The population explosion is greatest in non-Christian lands, so that by the very fact of human birth, we are losing the race daily. Add to this fact the surprising new vigor of the non-Christian religions. Zealously they are winning converts. Add to this distressing situation the many thousands in the world today who have recently learned to read through the Laubach literacy work in nations and tribes around the world. Who is giving these new readers literature to read? We Christians have been slow to respond, and the Communists are flooding these new readers with their propaganda, anti-Christian and anti-American. And now let us look at ourselves. Where is the zeal we should have, the faithfulness in giving and going and praying? No wonder we are the "dwindling minority"!

Lest we get too discouraged, let me remind you that God is still upon the throne and He has always counted on His *remnant* to do double duty. All through the Bible, it has been the faithful remnant who have carried the knowledge of God out into the world. You and I are called today to be in the ranks of the remnant through whom God will yet work in our generation.

The church has often been quite dead, but God has given her many resurrections. Like a new strong wind, His Spirit has broken down the prejudices and impasses of centuries. He has brought reformation, revival, ecumenicity and new heights of zeal. Thus in Acts 2:47 we read that the Lord *added* to their number day by day; in Acts 9:31 that the Lord *multiplied* the church in the comfort of the Holy Spirit. He did it then. He will do it again through the preaching and teaching and personal witnessing of the Word . . . and our oneness in *loving living*.

6—Committed Living

I believe in the forgiveness of sins

A man, not always too honest in his dealings but very regular in church attendance, once admitted, "The only part of the Apostles Creed which I can say and really mean is 'I believe in the forgiveness of sins.' Every Sunday I come to get my slate cleaned up. Then I feel good all over, and begin another busy week." Another man came to church once a year, to the Maundy Thursday Holy Communion service. At that time he "took care of" the year's accumulation of sins, and was seen no more until the next Holy Week.

What am I trying to say with these illustrations? Here were churchgoers who believed in the *need* and the *fact* of the forgiveness of sins, but who unfortunately never saw the *implication* of it.

Let us remind ourselves first that forgiveness of sins is the very essence of the Christian gospel. In the forgiveness of sins, the fellowship with God is highest and innermost. Without the forgiveness of sins we would have no Good News, no sacraments. Forgiveness of sins is more than a doctrine; it is a subjective experience as God Himself comes to us to give us this free gift out of pure mercy and fatherly compassion. This is an act of God through the Living Christ. He gives us this gift by which our guilt is erased and we are made free. He cleanses us from *all* unrighteousness (I John 1:9). The psalmist, having experienced this forgiveness, calls us to "Be glad in the Lord, and rejoice . . . and shout for joy" (Psalm 32:11).

Having thus experienced this great act of God, and assuredly believing that we are forgiven, what should our relationship be to this merciful God? This mercy, made possible on the cross of Calvary, calls for *total commitment* to Him who died there. A prayer and a hymn of thanksgiving are very acceptable to Him, but this should be accompanied by a life of walking worthy of the privilege of divine forgiveness.

George Matheson, in his poem, "O Love That Wilt Not Let Me Go," expresses his response to his Saviour in these words: "I give Thee back the life I owe." Cecil F. Alexander, in his hymn, "There Is a Green Hill Far Away," reminds us:

> O dearly, dearly has He loved,
> And we must love Him, too,
> And trust in His redeeming blood,
> And try His works to do.

What does this mean? It means that as each new day dawns, God meets man anew with the offer of forgiveness and His promise to be present to bless. One single day without renewal of forgiveness of sin, and thanksgiving, is sad neglect of so great a gift. If a man really accepts the offered forgiveness, deep gratitude will arise in his heart and his eyes will be opened to the dignity of the day's tasks before him. He now sees that it is God's will that he do his tasks "to the glory of God." Out of gratitude he will want to be faithful in even the smallest detail.

In his book *Our Calling*, the Swedish theologian Einar Billing puts it this way: "This is the task of continuously transforming these old, monotonous, unpleasant, interest-killing and soul-destroying duties into new and fresh and heartabsorbing interests." Thus the mother who rejoices in the forgiveness of sin begins the day in the name of Him who so graciously forgave her. If her fellowship with her Lord is real, her desire will be to do her housework, her child care, her purchasing—everything—well, knowing that her Redeemer sees and hears and knows all. Aware of His presence, she will not permit herself to do her work carelessly, grudgingly, or with divided interest. She experiences joy as she goes to her work as she would to worship.

Can the man who has thankfully accepted the forgiveness of his sins go back to his office and continue in unethical practices as before? Doesn't this make a mockery of his confession?

A student of mine once had a part-time job in an office. Imagine my chagrin one day when the employer called me on the telephone with this accusation: ". . . he attends a Bible School and calls himself a Christian, perhaps even thinks he is better than I am. Well, I'll tell you what! My other employee, who has no religious connection, is more faithful and dependable than your Bible-reading student." What a disgrace, when we who accept forgiveness of sin cannot be relied upon in the little duties and responsibilities entrusted to us!

But God offers more! Among the most wonderful gifts in the forgiveness of sins is this one, that God permits us poor children of the earth to become co-workers in His Kingdom. We are to help spread the knowledge of the availability of this forgiveness to our neighbor next door and in faraway places to tribes and peoples still untouched by this glorious Good News. We are to speak a word for Him to those who need His comfort and courage. We are to take a stand against evil. We are to help promote understanding and goodwill. We are to help build the Kingdom of kindness. What dignity this places upon our lives! We are to live redeemed.

A woman in her forties, a stranger to me, came into my office one day to discuss plans for her future. She had unusually hard, coarse lines in her face. Her fingers were brown from chain smoking. Her voice was hoarse. Love of the world and its lusts was imprinted on her face. But a change had taken place within her—someone had given her hope for a better life, had spoken to her of the availability of the forgiveness of all her sins. In faith still weak but nevertheless alive, she had permitted God to give her the undeserved, free gift of His forgiveness. She was inwardly clean. All the years of sin had been removed. She was free. Her gratitude was immense. She had to share her joy with someone, with anyone who would listen. But now the implication of the forgiveness also dawned upon her. How could she turn her back on her sinful past and enter in upon God's better plan for her? And so she came seeking counsel.

One thing, her hard face, still bothered her. To my amazement she affirmed presently, "God can change that, too. You watch; after a few months of right living, and with love in my heart, God will soften the lines in my face, and will take away my coarse voice. I firmly believe this!"

I have not seen her in years, but I am sure that the happiness of knowing she is redeemed will express itself on her face and in her voice. She will be radiant with *committed living*.

7—Eternal Living

I believe in the resurrection of the body and the life everlasting

What am I really saying when I say that I believe in the resurrection of the body and the life everlasting? Do these statements really reflect my faith in the fact that I shall one day rise again from the grave? As I give this affirmation some more thought, I realize I am saying something different from just "I believe in immortality." The Greeks of Paul's day also believed in a form of immortality, but to them the idea of a bodily resurrection was absurd. Paul, speaking at Athens, was ridiculed for his belief in the resurrection of the body. Writing to the Philippian Christians, he affirmed, "He will change our weak mortal bodies and make them like his own glorious body, using that power by which he is able to bring all things under his rule" (Philippians 3:21, TEV).

How precious are the words our Lord spoke to Martha at the death of her brother Lazarus: " 'I am the resurrection and the life; he who believes in me, though he die, yet shall he live' " (John 11:25). Or His earlier words: ". . . for the time is coming when all the dead in the graves will hear his voice, and they will come out of their graves: those who have done good will be raised and live, and those who have done evil will be raised and be condemned" (John 5:28-29, TEV).

It strengthens our faith when we read, "Brothers, we want you to know the truth about those who have died, so that you will not be sad, as are those who have no hope. We believe that Jesus died and rose again; so we believe that God will bring with Jesus those who have died believing in him. For this is the Lord's teaching we tell you: we who are alive on the day the Lord comes will not go ahead of those who have died. There will be the shout of command, the archangel's voice, the sound of God's trumpet, and the Lord himself will come down from heaven! Those who have died believing in Christ will be raised to life first; then we who are living at that time will all be gathered up along with them in the clouds to meet the Lord in the air. And so we will always be with the Lord. Therefore, cheer each other up with these words" (I Thessalonians 4:13-18, TEV).

In the great resurrection chapter (I Corinthians 15), Paul rests his whole argument for the resurrection of our bodies upon the undisputed fact of Christ's resurrection. "Knowing that He who raised the Lord Jesus will raise us also with Jesus and bring us with you into His presence. . . . So we are always of good courage; we know that while we are at home in the body we are away from the Lord, for we walk by faith, not by sight. We are of good courage, and we would rather be away from the body and at home with the Lord. So whether we are at home or away, we make it our aim to please Him. For we must all appear before the judgment seat of Christ, so that each one may receive good or evil, according to what he has done in the body" (II Corinthians 4:14, 5:6-10).

All of these Scriptural statements give us certainty that the resurrection of the dead is not something for which we wish but something which we *know* to be true. If this teaching were not true, our whole Christian faith would fall; His death would have been in vain. But thanks be to God, we are assured that because He rose from the dead, we too shall rise.

If we truly believe in the resurrection of the body and life everlasting, this belief should color our whole attitude to life. As we take this assurance with us into the situations of everyday life, we gain the point of view of eternity. We tell ourselves that whether life is long or short, each day must count for Christ. Each day also will bring us closer to the time of departure from this earthly life, and closer to the great day when we shall enter upon a new existence for which we have no adequate words, and which we can only describe as *"in* His presence." Every day left for this earthly sojourn is of tremendous importance. If we are going to serve, we had better get at it!

Most of all, this faith in the resurrection of the body should be our great comfort as we bed dear ones down in the earth, and also as we anticipate our own departure. Surely, all of us hate the thought of physical death. But if our eyes are on the opposite shore with all its wonder, we are lifted above the dread to a happy anticipation. Death has lost its sting. There is victory!

This anticipation, however, needs to be developed by living trustfully in the certainty of the resurrection. In other words, it is an art that needs to be learned, through faithful contemplation of Christ's promises, and a life of daily contact with Him with whom we expect to spend eternity. If we are strangers to Christ here, how can there be a happy looking ahead to our coming into His presence? Instead there is only dread.

Often I catch myself wondering how Paul could say, ". . . My desire is to depart and be with Christ . . ." (Philippians 1:23). How did Paul get that way? Each year I seem to understand this better. Paul had seen Jesus face to face and had conversed with Him (Acts 26:13-18). To see Jesus was to love Him. To love Him was to want to be with Him.

As you and I, too, see more of Jesus through quiet hours of Bible study and prayer, He becomes more and more precious, until a very real longing steals into the heart to see Him beyond the printed page—a longing to be with Him forever in *eternal living*.

II

TRUSTFUL SINGING

8—*The Overflowing Heart*

Trustful living finds expression in trustful singing. We sing because our hearts overflow. Our deep feelings of sorrow or joy find release in words spoken or sung.

The Bible says, ". . . Whatever is in the heart overflows into speech" (Luke 6:45, Living Gospels).

Many are the gatherings of Christians who have broken forth into the Doxology upon having experienced God's help and guidance:

> Praise God from whom all blessings flow!

When the train bearing Robert Kennedy's body was delayed, the silent, waiting crowds at many railroad crossings began to sing softly the "Battle Hymn of the Republic":

> Mine eyes have seen the glory of the coming
> of the Lord;
> He is trampling out the vintage where the grapes
> of wrath are stored;
>
> He hath loosed the fateful lightning of His
> terrible swift sword;
> His truth is marching on.
> **Glory! Glory! Hallelujah!**

At flag raising services, as Old Glory rises high over the earth, we proudly and prayerfully sing:

> God bless our native land;
> Firm may she ever stand,
> Through storm and night. . . .

The Old Testament psalmists wrote:

> . . . Shout to God with loud songs of joy!
> (Psalm 47:1)

> O sing to the Lord a new song;
>   sing to the Lord, all the earth!
> Sing to the Lord, bless his name;
>   tell of his salvation from day to day. . . .
> (Psalm 96:1-2)

Paul, writing to early Christians, said, "Let the word of Christ dwell in you richly, as you teach and admonish one another in all wisdom, and as you sing psalms and hymns and spiritual songs with thankfulness in your hearts to God" (Colossians 3:16). Today, too, a Christian may say, "My heart sings within me," and so he joins in hymns of faith and trust and thanksgiving.

But not all singing is trustful singing. It is very possible for us to sing a hymn without having a trustful relationship to Christ. We may enjoy the melody and the lilt of a song, without experiencing the truth of the words. I suppose that in almost every hymn there are verses and phrases we do not really understand. This bothers me, especially when I remember that Christ once said, " 'This people honors me with their lips, but their heart is far from me' " (Matthew 15:8). I don't want to make rash promises which I will not keep. I want to know what I am saying, and I want to mean it with my whole heart. Therefore, I have for

35

years checked on the meaning of hymn words, and I now invite you to do so with me.

My aim is to give you a number of *Biblical word pictures* which are full of comfort and certainty. They have lived through the decades because they have spoken peace to human hearts. I invite you to linger on these word pictures so that you, too, will have them in your memory when you need them.

9—The Mercy Seat

My God, how wonderful thou art,
Thy majesty how bright,
How beautiful thy mercy seat
In depths of burning light!
—Frederick William Faber

This hymn shows a wholesome combination of reverential fear of God and of trustful confidence. The writer knows whom he trusts, and knows that although He is the great One of awful purity, yet He is at the same time our Father. Faber writes about the *beautiful mercy seat* —what is he trying to signify by those words?

Exodus 25 describes Moses receiving from the Lord instructions for building the ark of testimony. The cover was to be a lid made of gold with two golden cherubim, one on either side, facing each other, with their wings spread out above, overshadowing the ark. In Jewish thought, cherubim occupy high rank among the angels of heaven. The Lord was often represented as throned between the cherubim. This golden throne of God was the place where the sins of the people were covered or forgiven, as the high priest sprinkled the blood of the sin offering on the mercy seat. The purpose of this mercy seat becomes clearer when we read in verse 22 that the Lord said, " 'There I will meet with you, and from above the mercy seat . . . I will speak with you. . . .' "

Strictly speaking, God cannot be said to dwell in one place more than in another, but a special place of worship becomes in a special sense a meeting place with God. Thus the prophet Isaiah wrote, "For thus says the high and lofty One who inhabits eternity, whose name is Holy: I dwell in the high and holy place, and also with him who is of a contrite and humble spirit . . ." (Isaiah 57:15).

The writer to the Hebrews tells us of the Old Testament tent, the Holy of Holies with the mercy seat, then elaborates on how much better is our approach to God through the blood of Christ (Hebrews 9). From the mercy seat of the Old Testament, God extended mercy to penitent sinners. In our New Testament worship, God extends mercy to us from the empty cross on which Christ shed His blood for our sins.

I believe the writer of this hymn was thinking of the double beauty of the mercy seat. The actual seat described in Exodus was beautiful in its golden splendor—but for us the greatest beauty of the mercy seat lies in its being the place from which God's mercy comes to us, the undeserved kindness of a loving Heavenly Father. When next you sing the words *mercy seat,* remember that the hymn writer was speaking of the place where God met His people and spoke with them.

> How dread are Thine eternal years,
> O everlasting Lord,
> By prostrate spirits day and night
> Incessantly adored!

Twice in Daniel 7, the prophet speaks of God as the *Ancient of Days.* The 90th Psalm gives us another glimpse into the eternal existence of God: "Lord, thou hast been our dwelling place in all generations. Before the mountains were brought forth, or ever thou hadst formed the earth and the world, from everlasting to everlasting thou art God. . . . For a thousand years in thy sight are but as yesterday when it is past" (vv. 1-2, 4). *Dread* is a word suggesting intense fear mixed with awe; for a believer, this awe is moderated by trust in God's love. Hence the hymn writer could write:

> O how I fear Thee, living God,
> With deepest, tenderest fears,
> And worship Thee with trembling Hope
> And penitential tears
>
> Yet I may love Thee, too, O Lord,
> Almighty as Thou art,
> For Thou hast stooped to ask of me
> The love of my poor heart.

Do you sing these words with that same trustful fear, or are they just words which leave you untouched? Your answer will depend upon your relationship with God, and how well you know Him.

The *prostrate spirits* who adore the Lord with faces downward in humility and submission are the cherubim and seraphim who serve God day and night. Perhaps the author's inspiration came from Isaiah's vision: "I saw the Lord sitting upon a throne, high and lifted up. . . . Above him stood the seraphim; each had six wings: with two he covered his face, and with two he covered his feet, and with two he flew. And one called to another and said: 'Holy, holy, holy is the Lord of hosts; the whole earth is full of his glory'" (6:1-3). Of the celestial beings described in Revelation 4 we read that they never cease to sing, "'Holy,

holy, holy, is the Lord God Almighty, who was and is and is to come!'" (v. 8), and that they fall down before Him who is seated on the throne and worship Him.

What an honor that even here, in our sinful state, we may join in the worship of Him upon the throne. And how wonderful to think of finally seeing Him face to face and joining in that heavenly song of praise and adoration!

10—The Martyrs' Call

All hail the power of Jesus' name!
Let angels prostrate fall;
Bring forth the royal diadem,
And crown him Lord of all!

Crown him, ye martyrs of your God
Who from His altar call;
Extol the stem of Jesse's rod,
And crown him Lord of all!

Ye seed of Israel's chosen race,
Ye ransomed of the fall,
Hail him who saves you by his grace,
And crown him Lord of all!

Let every kindred, every tribe,
On this terrestrial ball,
To him all majesty ascribe,
And crown him Lord of all.

Oh, that with yonder sacred throng
We at his feet may fall,
Join in the everlasting song,
And crown him Lord of all.

—Edward Perronet

Oh, that we could participate more adequately in the true art of adoration! I wonder sometimes if we really sing this song with the awe and reverence that is written into the words.

This is a hymn of adoration and praise. The origin of the word *adore* is from the Latin word *adorare* meaning to speak. In other words, when we adore God we speak to Him of how great He is. It is interesting that the words adore and adoration are not found in the Bible. Let's see how the concept of awe and reverence is expressed in the Scriptures.

In one of several wonderful throne scenes in the book of Revelation, adoration is dramatized in the following manners: Heavenly beings give glory and honor and thanks to Him who is seated upon the throne; they fall down before Him; they worship Him; they cast their crowns before the throne, singing that the Lord God is worthy to receive glory and honor and power.

Of special interest is the ever widening circle of beings invited to join in this act of worship in this hymn: angels, martyrs, saved souls, sinners, every kindred and tribe, and finally "yonder sacred throng." In another hymn, we seek to gaze and gaze on Him, and symbolically to bring our crown of self to Him and let Him be supreme Ruler of our lives. The words *royal diadem* symbolize kingly power and authority.

In the second stanza we meet an unusual group: martyrs who from His altar call. Who are they, and why under the altar? We read of them in the book of Revelation: "I saw under the altar the souls of those who had been slain for the word of God and for the witness they had borne" (6:9). These are martyrs who chose to suffer and die rather than give up their faith in God. They are safe in God's keeping, killed upon earth but alive in His presence. The term *under the altar* is probably used because in ancient animal sacrifices the blood, which was considered the seat of life, was poured out at the foot of the altar (see Leviticus 4).

In Genesis 4:10 we find a parallel thought when God says to Cain, " 'What have you done? The voice of your brother's blood is crying to me from the ground.' " In Revelation, the blood is crying from under the altar. Their call is not one for personal revenge, but for the total and final vindication of divine justice.

Millions in our generation have died for their faith, and before the end of our time there will be multitudes more, but when the number of martyrs is full, the end will come. Let us learn *now* to cast our crowns before Him in praise and wonder, and with happy anticipation sing, "O that with yonder sacred throng we, too, may fall at His feet and adore Him forever!"

11—Protective Wings

Under His wings I am safely abiding;
Tho' the night deepens and tempests are wild,
Still I can trust Him; I know He will keep me;
He has redeemed me, and I am His child.
Under His wings, under His wings,
Who from His love can sever?
Under His wings my soul shall abide,
Safely abide forever.

—William O. Cushing

This song presents a word-picture of wonderful security and confidence. The melody is pleasant, so many people enjoy singing it. My hope is that as the result of singing it, they are helped to live trustfully.

The picture is one of protecting wings. What a wonderful thought with which to begin and to close the day! The day's worries are wiped out as we remind ourselves that protecting wings are watching over us. How good, too, to begin a journey with this assurance which diminishes the size of each threatening fear. The hymn writer, William O. Cushing (1823-1902), tells us that this image helped him to trust when tempests were wild; it was a refuge in sorrow; it was enjoyment when he knew he was hidden till life's trials were o'er. Let us, just for today, carry this picture in our hearts. Tomorrow there will be another one. The Scriptures are full of them. Why don't we use them!

To fasten this picture firmly in your mind, let me refer you also to the hymn of Joachim Neander:

> Praise to the Lord,
>   who o'er all things so wondrously reigneth,
> Shelters thee under His wings, yea, so gently
>   sustaineth.

It is from the Scriptures that the source of this message comes: ". . . hide me in the shadow of thy wings" (Psalm 17:8). "How precious is thy steadfast love, O God! The children of men take refuge in the shadow of thy wings" (Psalm 36:7). "Oh to be safe under the shelter of thy wings!" (Psalm 61:4). " 'O Jerusalem. . . . How often would I have gathered your children together as a hen gathers her brood under her wings, and you would not!' " (Matthew 23:37).

From the picture of safety under the hen's wings, we now turn to the picture of safety under eagle's wings. Those who know eagles tell us that when little eaglets first attempt to fly, the parent bird hovers around them and beneath them so as to support them on expanded wings when the eaglets are exhausted. " 'Like an eagle stirs up its nest, that flutters over its young, spreading out its wings, catching them, bearing them on its pinions' " (Deuteronomy 32:11). "He will cover you with his pinions,

42

and under his wings you will find refuge" (Psalm 91:4).

In the song "Jesus, Lover of My Soul" we find the words: "Let me to thy bosom fly." There is a story behind these words. Charles Wesley, the evangelist and hymn writer, was once standing at an open window. Suddenly he was startled to see a hawk in swift pursuit of a skylark. The frightened little bird fluttered between the trees with cries of terror. The hawk came closer and closer and threatened to overtake its prey. Presently the lark seemed to see Charles Wesley standing, silently watching the crisis. It flew towards him, straight to his bosom. There it lay with its little heart pounding. Wesley placed his hand over the little bird and trustfully it laid its head against him. Wesley was deeply moved by this experience, and he thought how like the little bird we are when we come fluttering to Jesus in our fears. Being a poet at heart, the words of our hymn came to him:

> Jesus, Lover of my soul,
> Let me to thy bosom fly. . . .
> Cover my defenseless head
> With the shadow of Thy wing.

Another thought also comes to us from the Scriptures. In Exodus 19 we read that Moses went up to God, and the Lord called him out of the mountain saying, "Thus you shall say to the house of Jacob, and tell the people of Israel: "You have seen what I did to the Egyptians, and how I bore you on eagles' wings and brought you to myself. Now, therefore, if you will obey my voice and keep my covenant, you shall be my own possession among all peoples, for all the earth is mine, and you shall be to me a kingdom of priests and a holy nation" (vv. 3-6).

God expected His people, having experienced the sheltering wings of God's mercy and care, to obey Him and be loyal to Him in gratitude. This He expects of us too. When, in a difficult situation, you were wonderfully kept, healed, protected, guided, and supported, did you let this lead you to endless gratitude and to holy living? Or did you forget to say "Thank you," and go on your way unchanged?

In the Swedish folksong "Children of the Heavenly Father," author Caroline Sandell Berg (1832-1903) develops this thought. First she tells of the safety of the children of the heavenly Father; then she admonishes them to praise the Lord, no matter what He permits to come to them, because his purpose is to keep them pure and holy.

> Children of the heavenly Father
> Safely in His bosom gather;
> Nestling bird nor star in heaven
> Such a refuge e'er was given.
>
> God His own doth tend and nourish;
> In His holy courts they flourish.
> From all evil things He spares them.
> In His mighty arms He bears them.
>
> Praise the Lord in joyful numbers;
> Your Protector never slumbers.
> At the will of your Defender
> Ev'ry foeman must surrender.
>
> Though He giveth or He taketh,
> God His children ne'er forsaketh.
> His the loving purpose solely
> To preserve them pure and holy.

When Christians part from one another they often sing:

> God be with you till we meet again,
> 'Neath His wings protecting hide you.

As you send your children off to school, your sons off to war, your dear ones onto the dangerous highways, or wherever—put them in the protecting care of God. Ask that He may cover each one with His protecting wings. Then act as if He heard you! Thank Him!

12—Gifts From Above

We give Thee but thine own,
Whate'er the gift may be:
All that we have is thine alone,
A trust, O Lord, from thee.
—William Walsham How

"We give Thee but thine own"—when you sang those words, did you really think of the implications? Did you realize what you were singing?

First you were telling God that you actually believed that all you have is His alone. Is your life His? Is your body His? Are your children His? Are your food and clothing His? Are your silver and gold, your bank account and securities His? Are your farms, your fields, your crops His? You just said so!

James wrote, ". . . whatever is good and perfect comes to us from God . . ." (James 1:17, Living Letters). The psalmist David also said so: "The eyes of all mankind look up to You for help; You give them their food as they need it. You constantly satisfy the hunger and thirst of every living thing" (Psalm 145:15-16, Living Psalms).

The hymnist also reminds us that what we call our own is really only entrusted to us: "A trust, O Lord, from thee." When something is entrusted to us, it is placed in our care for a limited time, loaned to us. At the end of our use of it we must report back; we must give an account of how we administered what was entrusted to us.

In Old Testament days it was impressed upon God's people not only that all they had was a gift from God but also that part of it was to be returned during their lifetime as thank offerings to God. This could be done by bringing offerings to the temple, and by giving to the poor. Thus we read that the first fruits of their grain, of their oil and of the fleece of their sheep was to be brought to the temple (Deuteronomy 18:4), that they were to bring tithes and offerings (Malachai 3:8-10). Interesting commands were given by the Lord in regard to care of the poor (who would never cease) from the land. Those who owned land were not to reap the harvest to the very borders of the land, but were to leave grain along the edges and in the corners of the field for the poor to take. Not all grapes were to be gathered from the vineyards; some were to remain on the vines for the poor. Every seventh year, all debts of the poor were to be cancelled. In that year the land was not to be seeded; it was to be left idle, and what seeded itself was to be for the poor and for the wild beasts. The prophet Malachai called it robbing the Lord if the people did not bring the tithe (one tenth) to His house (Malachai 3:8).

When we come to New Testament days, we hear Jesus also say, "'For you always have the poor with you'" (Matthew 26:11), implying that we always have the opportunity and obligation to share with the poor. Zacchaeus said, "'. . . half of my goods I give to the poor'" (Luke 19:8). Paul, writing to the Roman Christians (Romans 15:25-29), said, ". . . I am going to Jerusalem with aid for the saints. For Macedonia and Achaia have been pleased to make some contribution for the poor among the saints at Jerusalem; they were pleased to do it. . . ." To the Corinthians he wrote: "Now concerning the contribution for the saints. . . . On the first day of every week, each of you is to put something aside and store it up, as he may prosper . . ." (I Corinthians 16:1-2).

In another hymn we sing, "Take my silver and my gold, not a mite would I withhold." I wonder if we could really say these words if we were aware of the unseen Presence with us. The generosity of the Macedonian churches was thus described: ". . . they gave according to their means . . . and beyond their means, of their own free will, begging us earnestly for the favor of taking part in the relief of the saints . . . but first they gave themselves" (II Corinthians 8:3-5).

For those who really would like to give like that, but who fear that they might later be in want because of it, Paul gives the following helpful counsel: ". . . he who sows sparingly will also reap sparingly, and he who sows bountifully will also reap bountifully. Each one must do as he has made up his mind, not reluctantly or under compulsion, for God loves a cheerful giver. And God is able to provide you with every blessing in abundance, so that you may always have enough of everything and may provide in abundance for every good work. . . . you will be enriched in every way for great generosity, which through us will produce thanksgiving to God, for the rendering of this service not only supplies the wants of the saints but also overflows in many thanksgivings to God" (II Corinthians 9:6-12).

And so it is with spiritual gifts, too: God can only fill whatever size measure we bring to Him. If you bring a small receptacle of faith to God, He will fill it; but if you bring a great receptacle of faith, He will fill that. Whatever you are ready for, is ready for you. God will meet you where you are and give you all that you are able to receive, and from this you can share.

Let us look at the words, "Take my moments and my days; let them flow in ceaseless praise." You have sung these words lustily in meetings. If a secret recording had

47

been made of all your own words during the last twenty-four hours, and was now played back, would we hear a flow of ceaseless praise?

Finally, let us look at the concluding words of the hymn: "Take my love . . . my will . . . my heart . . . myself, and I will be ever, only, all for Thee." Only after we have given our total self, in reverent dedication to Christ, can we give cheerfully of time, of skills, of things. Therefore the hymn begins with the most necessary ingredient: Take my *life*.

Then only will we realize that every good gift comes to us as a trust from Him. Then we will not deliberately withhold from Him our firstfruits and our tithes.

As Christmas approached one year, General William Booth of the Salvation Army was asked to prepare a Christmas message to be sent to his workers throughout the world. He knew from experience the blessedness of unselfish service. Wishing this for all his team, he sent just one word over the wires—*Others*. The desire to do something for others is the first test of our closeness to Jesus and to our oneness with Him.

13—The Knock at the Door

O Jesus, Thou art standing outside the fast-closed door,
In lowly patience waiting to pass the threshold o'er:
Shame on us, Christian brethren, His Name and sign
   who bear;
O shame, thrice shame upon us, to keep Him standing
   there!

O Jesus, Thou art knocking; and lo, that hand is
   scarred,

And thorns Thy brow encircle, and tears Thy face
have marred.
O love that passeth knowledge, so patiently to wait;
O sin that hath no equal, so fast to bar the gate!

O Jesus, Thou art pleading in accents meek and low,
"I died for you, my children, and will ye treat me so?"
O Lord, with shame and sorrow we open now the
door;
Dear Saviour, enter, enter, and leave us nevermore.

—William Walsham How

"Behold, I stand at the door and knock; if any one
hears my voice and opens the door, I will come in to him
and eat with him, and he with me" (Revelation 3:20).
The One who knocks is Jesus Christ, the ascended and
returning Lord. The door is the entrance to your heart.
The knocking can be heard only if there is some stillness,
because often it is only a still small voice.

The knocking may come in the form of the troubling of
your conscience; it may come in the form of good desires
and holy ambitions; it may come through Scripture reading, through the words of a hymn, or perhaps through the
admonition of parents or friends. It may come as a great,
shattering blow, upsetting your choicest plans; it may come
as a great good fortune. Always it is the dear Heavenly
Father wishing to visit you.

The hand which is knocking is the hand of love, nail-
pierced and scarred.

Because He will not force the door open, you must give
the invitation to enter. How do you do this? You do it
merely by *wanting Him,* by listening to His voice as you
read the Word, by telling Him in so many words, "Come
into my heart. I want you to be my Guest." Just wanting
Him is the opening of the door. He enters, and you know
He is there.

49

After entering, there is a time to eat together. In Oriental culture it is said that you know a person if you eat with him; then you cross over the invisible threshold from being an acquaintance into being a friend. Before the meal begins, you first must set the table. But what can you set before your heavenly Guest? You look around and finally admit, "Nothing in my hand I bring." The only dish you can set before Him is one filled with all your helplessness, your sin, and your failure. He understands and accepts it as your best offering. Then He performs a miracle: He transforms it into His dish full of forgiving mercy—all that you need and want, an overflowing measure. With a heart full of gratitude you now sing:

"Dear Saviour, enter, enter, and leave us nevermore."

14—The Mighty Rock

Beneath the cross of Jesus I fain would take my stand,
The shadow of a mighty Rock within a weary land;
A home within the wilderness, a rest upon the way,
From the burning of the noontide heat, and the
    burden of the day.

Upon that cross of Jesus mine eyes at times can see
The very dying form of One who suffered there for
    me;
And from my stricken heart, with tears, two wonders
    I confess:
The wonders of His glorious love, and my unworthiness.
              —Elizabeth C. Clephane

The hymn "Beneath the Cross of Jesus" has several lovely word-pictures conveying the thought of trust, like delightful resting places along a dreary, hot, country road.

Our first stop is beneath the cross. In our mind's eye we stop at Calvary with those who stood there on that first dark Friday; with the centurion, with Mary Magdalene and Mary the mother of James, with Salome, with John, the beloved disciple, and Mary, the Lord's mother. As we sing this hymn we are there with all of them, looking up at the sacred head, wounded, with grief and shame weighed down, scornfully surrounded with thorns; the sacred head, pale with anguish, with sore abuse and scorn. If we are totally honest, we find ourselves singing, "Thy grief and bitter passion were all for sinner's gain; mine, mine was the transgression, but Thine the deadly pain."

Only as we are aware of human sinfulness, and our own inability to live up to God's demands of purity and love, can these words have any meaning. As soon as they do, we can't help praying another hymn verse:

What language shall I borrow to thank Thee, dearest Friend,
For this Thy dying sorrow, Thy pity without end?
O make me Thine for ever; and should I fainting be,
Lord, let me never, never outlive my love to Thee.

The second stop on our way is at the mighty rock in a weary land. This, too, is a Biblical picture which can be found in Isaiah 32. Chapters 32-35 contain prophecies of hope and comfort. After having given a "woe" message to God's people, because instead of putting their trust in the Holy One of Israel, they had sought security in an alliance with Egypt, relying on Egypt's horses, chariots and horsemen for protection, Isaiah calls them to turn to Him from whom they had revolted and predicts that Assyria, the enemy whom they feared, would fall. Then Isaiah points to the source of real help: "Behold, a king will reign in righteousness, and princes will rule in justice.

Each will be like a hiding-place from the wind, a covert from the tempest, like streams of water in a dry place, like the *shade of a great rock* in a weary land" (Isaiah 32:1-2).

The hymnist seems to be telling us that when we realize what security we have in the efficacy of Christ's death on the cross, it is like the refreshing shade from an unmovable great rock, giving comfort and courage to us travelers on life's highway.

Again, it is like a *home in the wilderness* with protection from the burning noontide heat. The message of the cross cools off the guilt-seared conscience. Both pictures fill us with wonder at Christ's redeeming love and our worthlessness.

The third verse also gives us a thought upon which we want to linger—*the sunshine of His face*. Thus we sing: "I ask no other sunshine than the sunshine of His face." The face into which we look is one of grace. It shines upon us in forgiving love. This reminds us of the words of the benediction with which the priests were to bless the people: " 'The Lord bless you and keep you: The Lord make his face to shine upon you, and be gracious to you: The Lord lift up his countenance upon you, and give you peace. So shall they put my name upon the people of Israel, and I will bless them' " (Numbers 6:24-27).

To "make his face shine" means to smile. To "lift up his countenance" means to take notice of. This blessing gives the assurance of God's presence and favor. The face of the Lord is against evil doers, while the eyes of the Lord are toward the righteous (see Psalm 34:15-16). Peter, in his first letter, puts it this way: " 'For the eyes of the Lord are upon the righteous, and his ears are open to their prayer. But the face of the Lord is against those that do evil' " (I Peter 3:12).

When David had sinned grievously one of his prayers

was, "How long wilt thou hide thy face from me?" (Psalm 13:1), but when David made his great confession, his prayer was, "Hide thy face from my sins, and blot out all my iniquities" (Psalm 51:9).

Let us remember that when we come as sinners to the Saviour in total helplessness and trust, His face shines upon us as a father's upon his child. We then dare to expect His forgiveness, and the joy of His nearness and love. Just think how much our lips said to Him in our song. Has our heart said it too?

15—The Mended Flaw

O beautiful for spacious skies, for amber waves of grain
For purple mountain majesties above the fruited plain!
America! America! God shed His grace on thee,
And crown thy good with brotherhood from sea to shining sea.

O beautiful for pilgrim feet, whose stern impassioned stress
A thoroughfare for freedom beat across the wilderness!
America! America! God mend thine every flaw,
Confirm thy soul in self-control, thy liberty in law.

O beautiful for patriot dream that sees beyond the years,
Thine alabaster cities gleam, undimmed by human tears!
America! America! God shed His grace on thee
And crown thy good with brotherhood from sea to shining sea.

—Katherine Lee Bates

When the Israelites were in Babylonian captivity, their oppressors mockingly urged them to sing some of their quaint songs, their psalms of trust in their Jehovah God. Thus we read in Psalm 137:1-3: "By the waters of Babylon, there we sat down and wept, when we remembered Zion. On the willows there we hung up our lyres. For there our captors required of us songs, and our tormentors, mirth, saying, 'Sing us one of the songs of Zion.'" In answer to this request to sing for the entertainment and amusement of their enemies they replied, "How shall we sing the Lord's song in a foreign land?"

We in the United States are not captive in a foreign land, but we are captives, nevertheless, of enemies within our own land and in our own hearts. Corruption, violence, lawlessness, delinquency, unfaithfulness and frustration abound. The same question comes from our lips when we read our newspapers and hear our newscasts: "How shall we sing the Lord's song in such a situation?" We don't feel like singing. Our hearts are heavy within. We feel so helpless. The general sigh all around us is, "Isn't it terrible! But what can we do about it?" Let us Christians not give in to the echo of helplessness. Rather let us keep affirming, "Our help is in the name of the Lord, who made heaven and earth" (Psalm 124:8).

Thus we Americans sing of our beautiful land with spacious skies, waves of grain, purple mountains and fruited plains. With our lips we even admit that there are flaws for which we need God's grace, but then we so often go right on indulging self, and relying on human wisdom and power. Our singing becomes a mockery. Let us, who earnestly seek God's grace, make this national song a supplication, trustfully believing that the God of the nations hears each prayer and uses it to pour out His blessing and care upon our land! Remember again God's promise that the earnest prayer of *one* righteous person has great power in its effect (James 5:16). Now multiply this power by the millions of believing, praying Americans, and you will have to admit that there is hope.

In order to sing this song with more meaning, let us look at the flaws which the author mentions:

Broken brotherhood—in the anthem the thought reaches out beyond the fellowship of believers to all men who are to live in brotherhood. In a special way we think of the founding of this nation to which immigrants from all nations, seeking a better life, came bringing with them their contributions of culture, skills, and thrift for the making of this nation. We are reminded of the inscription on our Statue of Liberty in New York harbor, a gift of the people of France: "Give me your tired, your poor, your huddled masses, yearning to breathe free; the wretched refuse of your teeming shore, send these, the homeless, tempest-tossed, to me: I lift my lamp beside the golden door." These moving words were written by a Jewish immigrant, Emma Lazarus.

The concept of brotherhood is a basic one. Oneness and unity are a necessity for the well-being of a nation. The specific word *brotherhood* is not found in the Scriptures but the thought of living together as brothers is. Thus in Psalm 133:1 we find: "Behold, how good and pleasant it is when brothers dwell in unity!" We think of the Pilgrims making their pact to discuss both sides of every question and differ without scorn—they wanted unity in diversity. We think sadly of the years when the black man in our land was not treated as a brother, of the Indian upon whose land we encroached more and more until we finally, condescendingly allowed him to live on reservations. We think of churches and Christian groups in which color and nationality made a difference, excluding some and including others. Yes, America has an ugly scar, this flaw of broken brotherhood! We may admit that every good gift comes from God—our land and homes, our family and friends, science and the arts, industry and invention—but the hymnist reminds us that all this must be *crowned* by brotherhood.

Let us admit our flaw. Each of us, in one way or another, has added to this break, mostly by thoughtlessness and self-absorption. Let us now not continue in our unconcern, and let us ask God to make us aware of human need around us, especially the need for the acceptance and kindness which we can give anywhere, anytime.

Lack of self-control—we sing, "America, God . . . confirm thy soul in self-control. . . ." "This is a free country," we hear many say. What they mean is, "I am free to do as I please." Anyone who speaks thus needs to learn an expression which Paul uses in writing to the Corinthian Christians: *for the common good* (see I Corinthians 12:7). To the Philippians he wrote: "Do nothing from selfishness or conceit, but in humility count others better than yourselves. Let each of you look not only to his own interests, but also to the interests of others" (Philippians 2:3-4).

To each of us was given a personality, a capacity for friendliness, special skills and aptitudes which are to be used for the common good, to help build a fellowship. These may seem like empty, idealistic words but they will become power as soon as we give God the first place in our lives. He will inspire and empower us to serve for the common good. One of the fruits of the Holy Spirit is self-control (see Galatians 5:22). Therefore a good prayer is for the Holy Spirit to do His work in you daily, especially to give you self-control. He will make you willing to get involved, "for God did not give us a spirit of timidity but a spirit of power and love and self-control" (II Timothy 1:7). It is urgent that we tell the youth of our land of this power before they fall prey to the destructive lack of self-control, thinking it brings happiness when in reality it destroys them and the nation.

Lawlessness—what do we really mean when in the hymn we pray, "America, God . . . confirm . . . thy liberty in law"? Liberty is dependent on law and order. When these break down anarchy results, and liberty is gone. As a nation forgets the fact that government is of God, it ceases to respect its own national laws and law enforcement agencies. I find it important to learn from Scriptures that a law enforcer is a servant of God. Listen to these words written at a time in Roman history when a despot was upon the throne: "Let every person be subject to the governing authorities. For there is no authority except from God, and those that exist have been instituted by God. Therefore he who resists the authorities resists what God has appointed, and those who resist will incur judgment. For rulers are not a terror to good conduct, but to bad. Would you have no fear of him who is in authority? Then do what is good and you will receive his approval, for he is God's servant for your good" (Romans 13:1-4). Someone has said, "Before a nation becomes a nation of law breakers, it becomes a nation of Sabbath breakers." Let us respect God's laws, and then look upon our nation's laws as a gift from God in which we are to participate for the common good. When we see a police officer directing traffic, let us remember that he is a servant of God for the common good. When anyone in authority enforces the law, let us remember he is a servant of God.

Cities dimmed by human tears—these words remind us of ghettos: people huddled in shacks; human loneliness in large cities even among the affluent; unemployment with its suffering and boredom, poverty and despair.

Can it be that in this great land of ours there should be tears of despair? Ah, yes; the newspapers report it, our politicians promise to end it, those caught in it let us know through violence, marches, riots. Yes, to our shame, it is true—and we now have to admit it after years of trying not to see it. Now, it seems, America is awaking from her sleep and is beginning to dream of *alabaster cities*.

Alabaster is a hard, white substance which resembles marble but is softer and translucent. It is largely used in

Egypt for vases which are beautiful to behold. Bible readers will remember the word from the story of the woman of Bethany, who came to the home of Simon the Leper where Jesus was a guest at a meal. The woman, a sinner, brought with her an alabaster jar of very expensive ointment. Finding Jesus, she broke the jar and poured its contents upon Jesus' head. When some guests were indignant over this "waste," Jesus said, " 'Let her alone; why do you trouble her? She has done a beautiful thing to me. . . . She has done what she could; . . . wherever the gospel is preached in the whole world, what she has done will be told in memory of her' " (Mark 14:6-9).

What was the hymnwriter trying to say when she spoke of the patriot's dream of alabaster cities beyond the years in America? Patriots are citizens who love and zealously support their own country. These people want, and will work for, equality for all, the drying of tears of despair. These patriots may not be able individually to do great things, but as each one does as the woman in the story did—all he can—it will all add up to change and improvement.

When you sing of the alabaster cities of future America, you are obligating yourself to "do what you can" in your community, together with others. You may begin with a kind word, a smile of acceptance, a prayer, just caring—even singing this song as a prayer. But begin!

16—Glory Hallelujah!

Mine eyes have seen the glory of the coming of the Lord;
He is trampling out the vintage where the grapes of wrath
  are stored;

He hath loosed the fateful lightning of His terrible, swift
   sword;
His truth is marching on.

He has sounded forth the trumpet that shall never call
   retreat;
He is sifting out the hearts of men before His judgment
   seat;
O be swift, my soul, to answer Him; be jubilant, my feet!
Our God is marching on.

In the beauty of the lilies Christ was born across the sea,
With a glory in His bosom that transfigures you and me;
As He died to make men holy, let us die to make men
   free,
While God is marching on.

Glory, glory hallelujah!
His truth is marching on.

—Julia Ward Howe

Here is a hymn for which we seem to have a new ap-
preciation. Today we hear it sung in groups of all kinds.
We remember how it was sung at the funeral of Winston
Churchill, who loved it so much. More recently we witnessed silent crowds, patiently awaiting the train bearing
the body of Robert Kennedy, spontaneously beginning to
sing, "Glory, glory, hallelujah! His truth is marching on."

With awakened interest in this hymn, it is well for us
to give some thought to its origin and author, and more
than that to its deepest spiritual meaning. Let's prepare to
sing this hymn, aware of its relevance for today. Out of
yesterday's struggle it was born. In today's struggle it still
has something to say.

In the year 1861 newspaper headlines announced: "First
Shot Fired; Fort Sumter captured; Federal capital in
danger." There was bitter struggle and loss on both sides.

In this situation, two individuals had been deeply stirred to action, and ultimately became involved in the birth of this song—a man and a woman who hated slavery with their whole beings, and who dared to stand up and be counted. Who were these two people?

Let us go back to 1856. A political group which opposed the extension of slavery and favored the admission of Kansas as a free state became the Republican party. The new party denounced the Dred Scott decision by the Supreme Court—a decision which held that a slave or a descendant of a slave could not be a citizen, and therefore had no standing in the U.S. courts; also that slave owners could carry their slaves as property into any territory.

Two years later John Brown, an intense anti-slavery agitator in Kansas, thought he saw a weak spot in the slavery system. He thought of the possibility of a Negro insurrection, and was ready to help bring this to pass. Therefore, with a score of followers, he raided the U.S. Arsenal at Harpers Ferry and tried to involve the slaves in the neighborhood. His plan failed; he was captured, and hanged for treason. Although his plan involved civil war and destruction and his sentence was legally just, he was convinced that he was doing a great service to humanity. Public opinion in the North raised him to the rank of a martyr. From the deep feelings in human hearts there came forth the following words to an old tune:

John Brown's body lies a-mouldering in the grave;
His soul goes marching on.

The other person involved in the birth of this song is Mrs. Julia Ward Howe, author and reformer. Although she had six children to care for, she assisted her husband, Samuel Gridley Howe, in editing *The Commonwealth,* an anti-slavery periodical, and was active in the American

Woman's Suffrage Association and president of the American branch of the Women's International Peace Association.

The Civil War was raging. From her window Mrs. Howe saw the Massachusetts Volunteers marching to the railroad station in Boston, singing their favorite marching song: "John Brown's body lies a-mouldering in the grave; His soul goes marching on."

It was the Reverend James Freeman Clarke who had challenged Mrs. Howe, "Why don't you write some good words for that stirring tune?" On the night of November 18, troops marched in the street below her window. At the gray dawn of morning light the first lines of a poem began to come to her. She arose and wrote the words which seemed to come as a revelation from a source beyond herself. This poem sprang into being without conscious effort on her part, and although she felt humble in the presence of this miracle, she did not realize its importance, and she gave away her original copy to the first person who asked for it. She sent her corrected version to the *Atlantic Monthly*. It appeared in print in February, 1862, and was "somewhat praised." The *Atlantic Monthly* sent Mrs. Howe a check for four dollars.

In any other year, the song might have remained "somewhat praised" and been soon forgotten. But 1862 was a bitter year for the cause of freedom. There was failure everywhere. The song offered hope, a new determination, and the solemn acceptance of sacrifice. Soon the men in the army, and civilians at mass meetings, were singing it. The effect was magical. At a meeting in Washington people shouted, wept, and sang together, and above the applause was heard the voice of Abraham Lincoln exclaiming, while the tears rolled down his cheeks, "Sing it again!"

But where did Mrs. Howe receive the inspiration for the words of her poem? No doubt from the account in the book of Revelation, which tells of the second coming of

Christ. In Revelation 14:14-20, Christ is depicted as the Conquering One, coming on a white cloud and having a sharp sickle in His hand. A voice from heaven tells Him to put in His sickle and to reap, for the hour has come for the harvest of the earth. It is fully ripe.

So He who sat upon the cloud swung His sickle on the earth and clusters of ripe grapes were reaped. They were thrown into the great wine press of the wrath of God where the juice was trodden out.

This all is a figure of speech to picture the Victorious Christ coming for final judgment, to deliver and to destroy.

The word *trodden* is used because in oriental lands grapes were gathered into large vats and the juice was squeezed out as men trampled on them with their feet. The *vintage* refers to the crop of grapes grown and stored in a single season. Thus we can say, "This wine is of the 1968 vintage."

But the words *grapes of wrath* refer us to verse 19 where we read of the treading of the wine press of the wrath of God. Often in the Bible the imagery of a cup in God's hand suggests divine vengeance upon nations. They must drink of the cup of vengeance. For example: "For in the hand of the Lord there is a cup, with foaming wine, well mixed; and he will pour a draught from it, and all the wicked of the earth shall drain it down to the dregs" (Psalm 75:8). Significant too are the words of Jesus: "He who believes in the Son has eternal life; he who does not obey the Son shall not see life, but the wrath of God rests upon him" (John 3:36).

Thus the Bible depicts a spiritual conflict. The eternal power of God and of His sacrificed Son, Jesus Christ, are arrayed against all the hosts of hell. Christ symbolically wields the sickle to reap that harvest which is His; namely, to take His elect ones, the church, to heaven and to destroy the wicked (see Matthew 25:31-46).

In the hymn the separation or sifting of good and evil

is found in verse 2: "He is sifting out the hearts of men before His judgment seat." In Matthew 13:37-43 Jesus spoke, " 'He who sows the good seed is the Son of man; the field is the world, and the good seed means the sons of the kingdom; the weeds are the sons of the evil one, and the enemy who sowed them is the devil; the harvest is the close of the age, and the reapers are angels. Just as the weeds are gathered and burned with fire, so will it be at the close of the age. The Son of man will send his angels and they will gather out of his kingdom all causes of sin and all evil-doers, and throw them into the furnace of fire: there men will weep and gnash their teeth. Then the righteous will shine like the sun in the kingdom of their Father. He who has ears, let him hear.' "

Another time Jesus taught, "When the Son of man comes in his glory, and all the angels with him, then he will sit on his glorious throne. Before him will be gathered all the nations, and he will separate them one from another as a shepherd separates the sheep from the goats" (Matthew 25:31-32).

Now let us go back to the message of the hymn. What was Mrs. Howe trying to communicate to the people of her time and to us? Was she writing of the second coming and the final sifting of good and evil at that time? Or was she thinking of the sifting of good and evil in her day and ours?

Let us remind ourselves again of the evils of her day: strife between those who practiced slavery and those who sought to abolish it; a nation divided in a deadly civil war. Hence, she gives her call to arms: "As He died to make men holy, let us die to make men free." Each verse ends with a trustful affirmation: "His truth is marching on"; "Our God is marching on"; "While God is marching on." She was sure God was still on the throne and that truth and justice would ultimately win out. In the sifting, right would prevail and wrong would fail.

Perhaps we like this hymn so well today because we too need the confidence that God is still on the throne. We have said long enough, "But what can we do? It all looks so hopeless!" Not so! We, who have experienced how God can save and defend, need to be vocal and to meet hopelessness with trust. Our job is to make known God's stipulation as to when and how He can help: "But the people that do know their God shall stand firm and take action" (Daniel 11:32).

No clearer statement of God's demands can be found than those in II Chronicles 7:14: ". . . if my people who are called by my name humble themselves, and pray and seek my face, and turn from their wicked ways, then I will hear from heaven, and will forgive their sin and heal their land."

Because those who do not know this answer cannot save our nation, it is up to us to tell the message over and over again as Mrs. Howe herself encouraged: "O be swift, my soul, to answer Him; be jubilant, my feet!" *Hallelujah* means "praise the Lord." Give Him glory, great honor, worship, adoration, for He is working on in our behalf. Our God is marching on!